# APPARITIONS

# OF DEATH

# AND

# DISEASE

# THE GREAT
# HUNGER IN
# IRELAND

CHRISTINE KINEALY

# CONTENTS

*Malone: Me father died of starvation in Ireland in the Black '47.
Maybe you've heard of it.*

*Violet: The Famine?*

*Malone: No, the starvation.*

*When a country is full o' food, and exporting it, there can be no famine.*

George Bernard Shaw, *Man and Superman*, 1903

The above extract from a play by Irish-born playwright, George Bernard Shaw, written at the beginning of the 20th century, captures some of the meaning of the Great Famine to the generation that was born in its immediate wake. This issue persists today: how did a famine of such magnitude and severity occur in a country that was still exporting vast quantities of foodstuffs, and which, moreover, lay at the center of the resource-rich British Empire? The answer to these questions remains contested, and possibly unanswerable. Nonetheless, asking is central to understanding why so many people died or emigrated in the tragedy, simply remembered by Irish Americans as *An Gorta Mór*, or the Great Hunger.

Regardless of the impact and legacy of the Famine, this event was the subject of little scholarly research, artistic representation or public commemoration until the mid-1990s. For some historians, the Famine had come to represent a simple nationalist narrative of Irish history, which at its core was anti-British, and which they did not want to perpetuate. The onset of the Troubles in Northern Ireland after 1969 forced a number of reconfigurations in Irish politics and a renewed academic reluctance to engage with unpalatable aspects of Irish history.[1] This situation only changed in the mid-1990s, which also coincided with the commencement of the peace process. More books were written on the topic of the Famine in the two years after 1995 than had been written in the previous 150 years. It was not only scholars who broke the silence. The Famine became commemorated in music, literature (especially children's) poetry, art and sculpture. Prior to 1995, there had been few public Famine memorials, but the 150th anniversary of the tragedy was marked with permanent monuments being installed as far apart as North America and Australasia [Figure 1].

Figure 1 | John Behan, *The Arrival—The New Dawn*

5

The Irish, British and American governments all played a role in officially remembering the Famine. This culminated with a commemorative weekend in County Cork in May 1997, at which the then British Prime Minister, Tony Blair, read a brief statement that included a powerful acknowledgment of the wrongs that had been done to the Irish poor 150 years earlier: "Those who governed in London at the time failed their people" (*The Independent,* June 2, 1997).

More than two decades later, interest in the tragedy shows no sign of diminishing, with a profusion of ways of remembering and commemorating it. Scholarly and popular interest have also moved closer together, as was demonstrated when a 728-page *Atlas of the Great Irish Famine* (Crowley, Smyth, and Murphy, eds.) was named International Education Services Best Irish Published Book of the Year in 2012. The following account provides an overview of what took place in Ireland between 1845 and 1852. It seeks to convey both the complexity and the awfulness of Ireland's Great Famine, while bearing in mind the words of the cultural critic, Terry Eagleton, who said that "the event, like Auschwitz, continues to elude appropriate speech" (*The Observer Magazine,* February 20, 1994).

how did a famine of such magnitude and severity occur in a country that was still exporting vast quantities of foodstuffs ?

In late summer 1845, newspapers throughout Europe were carrying reports of a previously unknown disease that was destroying the potato crop from Belgium to England. By the end of August, the disease had reached Ireland. On September 13, London newspaper the *Gardeners' Chronicle and Gazette* responded to this news by announcing: "We stop the presses with great regret to announce that the potato Murrain has unequivocally declared itself in Ireland. The crops about Dublin are suddenly perishing. Where will Ireland be in the event of a universal potato rot?" At this stage, no one expected that this mysterious disease would reappear, with varying degrees of ferocity, for a further six years. The answer to the ominous question posed by the London newspaper could have been, "Ireland will starve" [Figure 2].

Figure 2 | John Behan, *Potatoes: Famine*

# IRELAND BEFORE 1845

Potatoes were not native to Ireland, but had been introduced to the country from South America in the late 16th century, initially as a food for the wealthier classes. The vegetable proved well-suited to Irish conditions, and was even able to flourish in areas that were rocky and contained poor soil. As a consequence, potatoes moved from being part of the diet of the middle classes, to being the subsistence food of the poor. Centuries of dispossession and discrimination against the native Catholics by successive British rulers and governments had created an underclass that was politically, economically and culturally disadvantaged. For these people, potatoes increasingly provided a lifeline that allowed them to exist on small plots of rented land, with few material resources.

In the century preceding 1845 there had been intermittent crop failures in Ireland. Earlier seasons of food shortages had been eased with a combination of private and public charity.[2] Consequently, with the exception of the famine of 1740–41—the notorious *Bliain an Áir* or "Year of Slaughter"—mortality levels had been contained.[3] While the potato crop did fail intermittently in the late 18th century, dependence on this single crop continued to increase, with more and more land, especially poor-quality land in the west, being brought under cultivation. The depression that followed the end of the Napoleonic Wars in 1815, increased dependence on the potato even further (Feehan 28–29). By 1845, at least one-third of the population depended almost solely on this vegetable for subsistence, while potatoes were also widely consumed by other members of the poorer classes—agricultural and industrial—whose livelihood was both liminal and precarious.

The Irish population had grown rapidly, more than tripling in the century that followed the 1741 famine, reaching more than 8 million by the time of the 1841 census (Kennedy and Clarkson 158–65). The size and rapid increase of the Irish population proved to be a concern to successive British governments, as poverty and population growth had become indelibly linked largely due to the writings of a prominent political economist, Rev. Thomas Malthus. The high dependence on the ubiquitous potato was viewed in Britain as a major cause of Irish poverty, overpopulation and economic backwardness. Malthus himself had warned a parliamentary committee, sitting in 1826 and 1827, of the potential dangers of Irish population increase for Britain, suggesting that the political Union between the countries could prove to be disadvantageous to the British people:

*It is vain to hope for any permanent and extensive advantage from any system of emigration which does not primarily apply to Ireland, whose population, unless some other outlet is opened to them, must fill up every vacuum created in England and Scotland, and to reduce the labouring classes to a uniform state of degradation (Report of the Select Committee 312).*

However, regardless of widespread poverty, Ireland did not appear to be a country about to undergo a sustained and deadly subsistence crisis. While dependence on a single crop, the potato, was high, growth of this vegetable had a number of advantages. It was prolific and extremely nutritious (especially when consumed with buttermilk), and it enabled the concurrent cultivation of grain, much of which was grown for export. In addition to human consumption, potatoes were used to feed pigs, cattle and other livestock.

"We stop the presses with great regret to announce that the potato Murrain has unequivocally declared itself in Ireland."

The appearance of a new strain of potato disease throughout Europe in the summer of 1845 was initially regarded with dismay, but not alarm. Periodic crop failures were not unusual and damage to the corn or potato crops rarely lasted for more than one year. Even within Ireland, the expectation was that the potato disease would result in food shortages, but not famine. Since the passage of the Act of Union in 1801, Ireland had been governed from Westminster in London. Despite being part of the newly created United Kingdom, Ireland continued to be treated as a colony.[4] Moreover, Catholics, the majority population in the country, had remained excluded from full political participation in this parliament until the granting of Catholic Emancipation in 1829. The condition of Ireland, its people and its land, was well-known to the government and administrators in London as a result of a number of detailed inquiries undertaken in the 1830s and 1840s.

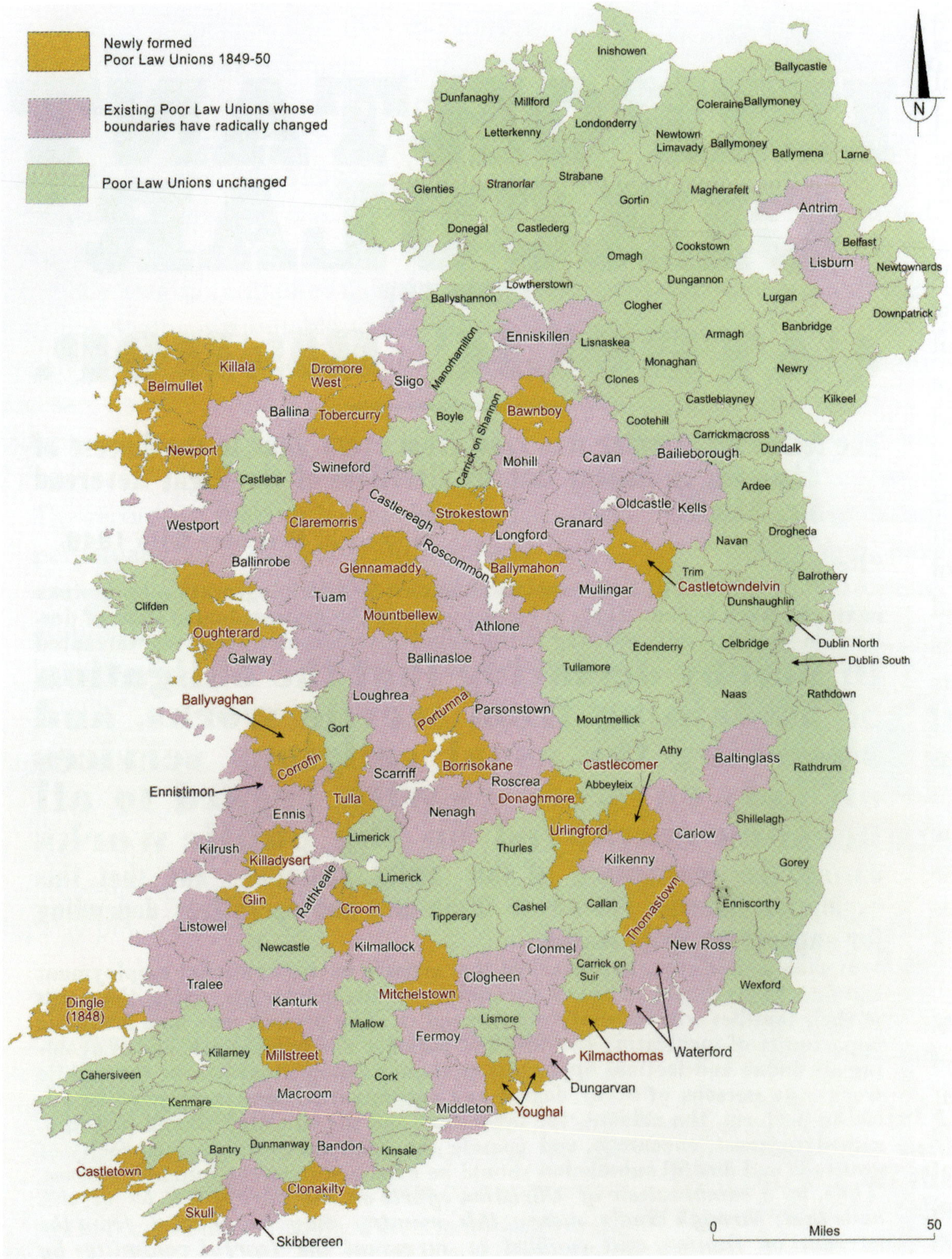

**Figure 3** | "Map of Poor Law Unions" (*Atlas of the Great Irish Famine, 1845–52*)

A major investigation into Irish poverty, which had taken three years to complete, had been followed by a smaller inquiry to consider the suitability of having a Poor Law in Ireland, modeled on relief provision in England and Wales (Kinealy, *Charity* 38–40). It was conducted by an Englishman, George Nicholls, who had little previous knowledge of Ireland. The outcome was the introduction of an Irish Poor Law in 1838, which divided the country into 130 Poor Law Unions **[Figure 3]**. Each union had its own workhouse and, architecturally, these were designed to be forbidding. All relief was to be provided within these institutions, which acted as a physical embodiment of the intended harshness of the system. Every workhouse was to contain an infirmary, although they were only to be for the use of sick inmates, not the general public. The day-to-day running of the workhouses was managed by paid staff who, in turn, were appointed by an elected board of Poor Law "Guardians." In a number of ways, therefore, the Irish poor were better served than the poor in many other European countries. Significantly, however, Nicholls, who was responsible for introducing the poor law system to Ireland, had warned that a self-financing Poor Law would not be suitable to deal with a period of famine on the grounds that, "[w]here the land has ceased to be reproductive, the necessary means of relief can no longer be obtained from it, and a Poor Law will no longer be operative" (357). His advice was ignored after 1845.

By 1845, 118 of the planned 130 workhouses were providing relief. The deterrent aspect that was integral to the new institutions appeared to be working as they contained few inmates.[5] Overall, the Irish Poor Law and the debates that preceded it demonstrated the unsympathetic and inflexible attitude of the British government toward Irish poverty. The insistence that Irish property should support Irish poverty proved to be a particularly cruel doctrine during any period of sustained food shortages. Moreover, by making the Irish Poor Laws far more stringent than the English and Scottish Poor Laws, a point was made that Ireland was not regarded as an equal partner within the United Kingdom.

# THE ONSET OF THE GREAT HUNGER

Potato blight was first detected in Ireland in late August 1845. It arrived relatively late in the harvest period and its appearance was irregular, with less than 50 percent of the crop being destroyed. The British government, under the leadership of Sir Robert Peel, responded promptly to the news, putting in place a number of relief measures, which included the importation of Indian corn. These arrangements were intended to operate alongside the Poor Law, and were intended to be short-term only. A scientific commission was established to investigate the cause and remedies for the mysterious disease. Its reports demonstrated how little people, even leading scientists, understood about the nature of the blight. Some attributed its spread to atmospheric factors solely, while remedies for preserving the seed potatoes ranged from soaking in a saline solution to sprinkling with either sulfuric or hydrochloric acid. Nothing, however, proved efficacious. Nonetheless, the relief measures proved successful, with little or no excess mortality occurring in the year following the 1845 harvest.

while dependence on a single crop, the potato, was high, growth of this vegetable had a number of advantages. It was prolific and extremely nutritious

An unforeseen consequence of the potato blight was that it precipitated the downfall of the British Prime Minister. In June 1846, Sir Robert Peel used the food shortages in Ireland to remove the protective tariff on corn imported into the United Kingdom.[6] Peel's actions did not have the support of many within his own Conservative party, who saw it as a betrayal of the landed interest, and he was forced to resign as Prime Minister. Peel was replaced by Lord John Russell, leader of the Whig Party—a party generally regarded as being more sympathetic to Ireland. Consequently, at a time of crisis in Ireland, British politics were in disarray. Divisions were also taking place in Irish politics. The Repeal Party, which had agitated for a parliament in Dublin, was also in turmoil. Its leader, Daniel O'Connell, at age 70, was physically and mentally declining and had lost the support of many in his party. He died in May 1847 in Genoa, Italy. His final speech in the British parliament had been a poignant plea on behalf of the poor in Ireland. At a time when Ireland needed strong representation and leadership, politics in Britain and Ireland were weak and fractured. Worrisome also, as these divisions were taking place, the blight was making its second, more extensive, appearance in Ireland.

the reappearance of the potato blight in the summer of 1846, earlier in the season and in a more virulent form, transformed the temporary food shortages into a major subsistence crisis

Few, if any, had died of starvation during the first year of food shortages in Ireland. However, the reappearance of the potato blight in the summer of 1846, earlier in the season and in a more virulent form, transformed the temporary food shortages into a major subsistence crisis. The second potato blight resulted in the destruction of more than 90 percent of the crop. Apart from the magnitude of the loss, the cumulative effect of a second year of shortages left the poor with few resources, either bodily or materially. Faced with this woeful situation, the widespread expectation was that the new Whig government would intervene to compensate for the shortages. This hope seemed to be realized when Lord John Russell informed the House of Commons on August 17, 1846 that he would employ the "whole credit of the Treasury ... to avert famine and maintain the people of Ireland" (*Hansard* 1846: 772–78). In retrospect, it was a hollow promise.

Several members of the new Whig government regarded the relief measures of the previous year as having been too generous and suggested that Irish reports of suffering had been embellished. Continuity was provided in that the Treasury was to again oversee the new relief measures. Charles Trevelyan, the principal civil servant at the Treasury, was given a primary role in administering assistance to Ireland. Unfortunately for the Irish poor, Trevelyan allied himself with a "moralist" circle in British politics who viewed the food shortages in providentialist terms.[7] Simply put, they suggested that the food shortages and consequent famine were God's will. Trevelyan's brusque manner and dogmatic approach were disliked by others involved in the relief operations.[8] Nonetheless, he had a number of powerful allies. The new Whig Chancellor of the Exchequer, Sir Charles Wood, shared Trevelyan's providentialist view of the Famine and, together, they were able to ensure a stringent and minimalist approach to the giving of relief. As a consequence, the lives of many Irish poor had become dependent on one civil servant in London, and the machinations of a weak and divided government at Westminster.

Irish and British merchants showed more interest in using the food shortages as a way of maximizing their profit, rather than getting food to the poor and starving

Despite the large shortfall in food production following the second potato failure, the new Whig government decided not to intervene in the marketplace, but to leave food supply to market forces. Even Peel's limited interventions in the previous year had angered merchants and proponents of free trade. However, a number of restrictions on the importation of foodstuffs remained and a sharp increase in freight charges added to the cost of bringing food into Ireland. Moreover, both Irish and British merchants showed more interest in using the food shortages as a way of maximizing their profit, rather than getting food to the poor and starving. A leading Whig politician, Lord Bessborough, privately expressed his frustrations to the Prime Minister, informing him that the merchants had done "as little as they could" to bring food to Ireland. At the same time, they had "done their best to keep up prices" (*Russell Papers,* January 23, 1847).

# BLIGHT RETURNS

The Whig government decided that public works, based on hard physical labor, were to be the main means of providing relief in the second year of food shortages. There were a number of changes from the way in which they had operated in the previous year, which made them little suited to the needs of a hungry and weak people. As far as possible, the daily rate of pay was based on output, which disadvantaged people who were already feeble. The works undertaken—usually roads or walls built in out-of-the-way places—were to serve no function, except to act as a test of destitution. Regardless of widespread distress, the public works proved slow to become operative, causing further hardship. But even as the works got underway, they proved inadequate for the demands being placed on them. One consequence was that the workhouses started to fill; as early as November, for example, the Sligo Union stopped making further admissions (*The Nation,* November 27, 1846). The large number of workhouse inmates put pressure on local ratepayers, especially in areas where they were being called upon to finance other forms of relief. Inversely, therefore, the poorest areas were paying the highest amounts of taxation. By the end of the year, many workhouses were full and not able to admit any more people, and the Irish and British newspapers were daily carrying stories of disease, dislocation and death. Famine had come to Ireland.

Originally the public works had been intended for men, but by the end of the year women were seeking employment on them. Visiting Quaker, William Bennett, observed:

*It was melancholy and degrading in the extreme to see the women and girls withdrawn from all that was decent and proper and labouring in mixed gangs on the public roads. Not only in digging with the spade, and with the pick, but in carrying loads of earth on their backs, and wheeling barrows like men, and breaking stones, are they employed. My heart often sank within me ...* (Bennett 9).

Even those who gained employment still suffered hardship. The hard physical demands made upon hungry bodies, combined with low wages and scant clothing, had disastrous results. Dysentery (also known as "the flux"), resulting in severe diarrhea, was one outcome. The low wages, at a time of high food prices, also undermined the effectiveness of public works. Additionally, many thousands were too infirm to seek employment. In these cases, private charity came to the assistance of those who fell outside the limited relief being provided by the government. Charity was propping up the official relief measures, but even this combination was not enough to save lives.

physical demands made upon hungry bodies, combined with low wages and scant clothing, had disastrous results

While no part of Ireland escaped the ravages of famine, the suffering of two small towns in West Cork, Skibbereen and Schull, embodied the failure of government relief. By November 1846, deaths in Schull were averaging 25 a day, and the number was rising. A local magistrate, Nicholas Cummins, who visited Skibbereen, felt compelled to write to the Duke of Wellington, describing the condition of the people. A copy of his letter was published in the London *Times* on Christmas Eve 1846. *The Illustrated London News* employed the artist James Mahony to go to the area and to visually capture the suffering for their readers [Figure 4]. His images provided a moving insight into communities devastated by famine, but he was aware of the limitations of such representations, and he declared that neither pen nor pencil could portray the full extent of the horror that he witnessed in Skibbereen (*The Illustrated London News,* February 13, 1847). As a consequence of this and other publicity, the small towns of Skibbereen and Schull achieved a grim notoriety internationally. One outcome was that private donations for the local poor were raised from within Ireland and further afield. For many, though, this charity proved to be too little and too late.

By the beginning of 1847, it was clear that the public works had failed. Administrative difficulties, the high cost of overseeing the system, and the consequent neglect of the land resulted in the works being brought to an end. Overall, they had proved to be more expensive and more difficult to administer than expected; they had also prevented small tenants who required relief from farming their own plots of land. Despite these shortcomings, the low pay they offered, the back-breaking labor they required, and the harsh reality that thousands died while working on them, the public works had never kept up with the demand for employment, and together with private charity, did provide a tenuous lifeline to millions of people during the winter of 1846–47.

**Figure 4** | "The Central Soup Depot, Barrack-Street Cork" (*ILN*, March 13, 1847)

The inadequacy of the relief measures to prevent high mortality was also causing dismay among the wealthier classes in Ireland. Regardless of political differences, in January 1847, a meeting of "peers, members of Parliament, and landed proprietors" was held in Dublin. Those who attended were deeply critical of the policies of the British government, particularly the fact that massive amounts of food were being exported. A number of resolutions were agreed upon, which were then embodied in a "Memorial" to the government. These included:

5. *That we recommend that Relief Committees should be allowed to sell food under first cost to the destitute, in their respective neighbourhoods, and that their doing so should not disentitle them to Government contributions in aid of their funds.*

6. *That while we affirm, that it is the clear and paramount duty of the State to take care that provision be made for the destitute, we regret that the means hitherto adopted for that purpose have, on the one hand, proved incommensurate with the evil, and on the other hand, have induced the expenditure of vast sums of money upon useless or pernicious works* (The Nation, January 15, 1847).

The meeting also agreed that the Famine should be met from the resources of the British Empire. The coming together of the Irish elites in Dublin on behalf of the poor in this way was unique and therefore significant. However, decisions regarding relief provision were being made 300 miles away in London, in Westminster and Whitehall. No account was taken of the recommendations that were made in Dublin.

# BLACK '47

At the beginning of 1847, the British government announced that the public works were to be brought to an end. Instead, a series of relief measures were to be introduced that would lead to the Poor Law becoming responsible for all relief in Ireland. In the intervening months, government soup kitchens would be opened. Yet, even after the closure of public works had been announced, the numbers employed on them continued to increase, reaching 734,000 in March 1847. The Treasury, anxious to bring this expensive relief project to an end, announced in March that there would be a minimum 20 percent reduction in people employed, to be swiftly followed by further reductions. The deliberate decision to close the public works ignored the fact that dozens of letters had been sent to the Treasury in the early months of 1847, by officials providing relief, outlining the starving condition of the people, even of those employed on the works. Increasingly, decisions being made in London bore no relation to the eyewitness testimony of officials working in Ireland or to the accounts of death from starvation or famine-related diseases that appeared in the press daily.

The closure of the public works at a time when many soup kitchens remained inoperative meant that there was a hiatus in the provision of government relief. The decision was condemned throughout Ireland. The Grand Jury in County Kerry described the Treasury's decision as equivalent to signing a "death warrant" on the poor of Ireland (*Times*, March 24, 1847). In the absence of official relief, it was left to private resources to fill the starvation gap. For Count Paweł Strzelecki of the British Relief Association, the impact of the sudden closure of the public works was to increase demands made on charitable resources. Throughout April, he doubled the grants that he was making available to local Poor Law officials.[9] In the absence of government relief, therefore, private charity was the only buffer between life and death. The Society of Friends, who had established their own charitable body at the end of 1846, were pessimistic that even when the government soup kitchens opened, their involvement would still prove to be necessary:

*From the present aspect of things around us, we cannot venture to anticipate an early termination or even diminution of our labours, but must rather contemplate increasing claims for help for several months to come, in consequence of the continued impoverishment of those classes bordering on the wholly destitute, whose means of support are abridged by the failure of employment, arising from the non-consumption to so large an extent of the ordinary products of their industry.*[10]

The Soup Kitchen Act, which provided for the establishment of soup kitchens and the distribution of food to the poor, was a new departure for the British government. Their introduction caught the imagination of a French society chef, Alexis Soyer, who lived in London. By 1847, Soyer had achieved celebrity status, not only for the recipes he served up to the rich and powerful, but also for his pioneering ergonomic use of kitchen space and his interest in devising nutritious recipes for the poor. He initially traveled to Dublin sponsored by private subscriptions, but his services were retained by the British government. His aim was to create both soup recipes and a custom-designed soup kitchen, to help ensure that the relief would be provided in the most efficient and economical way possible. On April 5, 1847, Soyer's "model" soup kitchen was opened in Dublin, amidst great fanfare. The dignitaries who attended the grand opening, perhaps inevitably, pronounced the soup to be "delicious" (*Dublin Evening Mail,* April 7, 1847). For those less fortunate, Soyer's soup would be their only means of survival in the months until the new harvest.

more than 3 million people were receiving free daily rations of food ... making it the largest relief scheme ever mounted in Ireland

By July 1847, more than 3 million people were receiving free daily rations of food from the soup kitchens that covered the country, making it the largest relief scheme ever mounted in Ireland. While mortality rates did slow down during the summer, the health of many of the poor remained fragile. A British Relief Association agent reported on May 1, 1847 that the poor in Arklow, "do not look so well as they did when I was here last; many of the old people as well as the young are dropping off; they have generally a paler and more sunken appearance, and more cases of swollen ankles" (*Report of the British Relief Association* 127). Asenath Nicholson, an American philanthropist and abolitionist, who was traveling through Connaught in the summer of 1847, was dismayed by the scenes she witnessed on a daily basis, writing: "I could scarcely believe that these creatures were my fellow-beings. Never had I seen slaves so degraded."[11]

In the wake of the second failed potato crop, a massive fund-raising venture commenced throughout the world on behalf of the Irish poor—often led by people who had no direct connection with Ireland. The two largest committees were managed by the Society of Friends in Dublin and the British Relief Association, which had headquarters in London. Private charity did not merely coexist alongside government relief, at times it came to the rescue of the latter. For example, when government soup kitchens were opened in the summer of 1847, the large cauldrons or soup pots that were required to accomplish such a large-scale relief program were only made available through the intervention of private charities.[12] Private charity also provided vital relief to children, much of it being distributed by voluntary women's committees. Individual women came to the assistance of the Irish poor and proved indefatigable in their efforts. The writer Maria Edgeworth, for example, received donations of money from groups in Australia, America and Britain, which she used to provide food and brogues (shoes) to the poor in her area.[13] By the autumn of 1847, private charity had largely dried up and so the poor, now facing a third year of shortages, were once again dependent on the government for assistance. While

**Figure 5** | Margaret Lyster Chamberlain, *The Leave-Taking*

private charity undoubtedly saved many lives, its involvement was sometimes tarnished by the activities of a small number of proselytizers, who used the hunger of the Catholic poor as a way of converting them to Protestantism through promises of soup and eternal life. The activities of these evangelicals were condemned at the time, but the existence of "souperism" cast a long, dark shadow on the memory of private relief.

Throughout the Famine, the role of eyewitness testimonies from visitors to Ireland proved invaluable in raising public awareness of the need for more aid, but also to counter accusations of exaggeration that had been appearing in sections of the British press. Elihu Burritt, an American philanthropist, pacifist and abolitionist, who was traveling on foot in the southwest of Ireland, sent frequent reports to the American press of what he described as "apparitions of death and disease." He added: "Were it not for giving them pain, I should have been glad if the well-dressed children of America could have entered these hovels with us, and looked upon the young children wasting away unmurmuringly, by slow, consuming destitution" (*New York Christian Advocate* July 21, 1847). The suffering of young children was a sight many observers found to be particularly painful.

For increasing numbers of people, emigration provided an escape from the horrors of disease and death.

For increasing numbers of people, emigration provided an escape from the horrors of disease and death. While emigration cut across all social classes, in reality the very poorest classes could not afford to leave, the cost of the passage to North America (the favorite destination) proving too high. Moreover, those whose health was already depleted did not have the physical resources to endure the rigors of a long sea voyage. Most emigration was self-financed, but a number of landlords did provide funding, seeing it as a way of clearing their estates and getting rid of poor who represented a long-term tax burden. The callousness with which this was sometimes carried out led to many criticisms.[14] If emigration started as a voyage of survival, for thousands it ended in disappointment, with as many as 10 percent of people not making it to the new world. However, as almost 2 million people left Ireland in the decade after 1846, the numbers who arrived in America were still enormous, representing one of the largest ever movements of people. An unlooked-for consequence of the mass emigration was that Irish culture and Irish politics were transplanted to the towns and cities of North America, where they both flourished [Figure 5].

# THE CHANGING FACE OF FAMINE

Throughout the summer of 1847, there were reports that abundant crop yields were expected in the approaching harvest (*The Nation,* July 21, 1847). Although the area under potato cultivation was much smaller than usual, corn crops were predicted to be more plentiful than ever before. This prediction gave hope that there would be enough food for all those who had survived until that time. Encouraged by this news, in August 1847, the British government announced that the Irish Famine was over. They further announced that if any more relief was required, it had to come from Irish, not British taxation. This change-over was facilitated by the introduction of the Poor Law Extension Act, under which both permanent and extraordinary relief were to be consolidated. The Act also provided for 30 additional workhouses to be built and, for the first time, for relief to be provided outside of the workhouses (Poor Law Act, 1847). Clearly, the Famine was not over as, in 1848, more than a million people turned to the Poor Law, and its minimal form of relief, for survival. This announcement by the government effectively marked the end of most of the fund-raising activities that had taken place over the previous year, and it consolidated relief provision under one system. From the perspective of the government, the transfer of all relief to the Poor Law meant that Irish taxpayers were now solely responsible for financing Irish relief.

The burden for financing both the Soup Kitchen Act and the amended Poor Law fell primarily on owners of land, especially on landlords who owned estates containing many small occupiers. The large number of absentee landlords in many of the poorest districts exacerbated the difficulties of providing relief and of collecting the local taxes necessary to fund it. The response of landowners who were resident, varied greatly. Newspapers in County Mayo, for example, praised the actions of individual landowners, in particular the many interventions by Lord Sligo and his family (*Connaught Telegraph,* July 22, 1846). By 1848, however, there were evictions on their Westport Estate, although Lord Sligo claimed that he did so only out of economic necessity, and with careful selection.[15]  **[Figure 6]**.

In contrast, Sir Roger Palmer, who owned estates in Belmullet, also in County Mayo, achieved a grim notoriety for the heartless way in which his tenants were evicted, leading a local newspaper to describe him as "monstrous" (*Connaught Telegraph*, July 5, 1848). Undoubtedly, as the Famine progressed and the fiscal burden on occupiers of land increased, even benign landlords came under financial pressure. One outcome was large-scale evictions, which meant that homelessness, combined with hunger, became a major source of mortality after 1847 **[Figure 7]**. If some landlords behaved badly, they were not the only group to take advantage of the vulnerability of the poor. Food contractors and merchants sometimes exploited the situation. In Ballinrobe, for example, the Poor Law Inspector Dr. Dempster actually re-weighed the food that was being sold to the local people by local merchants. He found that in many cases the amount fell short of the amount paid for—sometimes by almost four pounds. The inspector suggested that this practice was widespread and that all merchants involved should be "indicted for fraud."[16] No action appears to have been taken as the same inspector was still reporting on similar incidents in the months that followed.[17] These incidents reveal that even when relief was being given, the circumstances of the poorest and most vulnerable members of society were fraught with difficulties, as societal ties broke down.

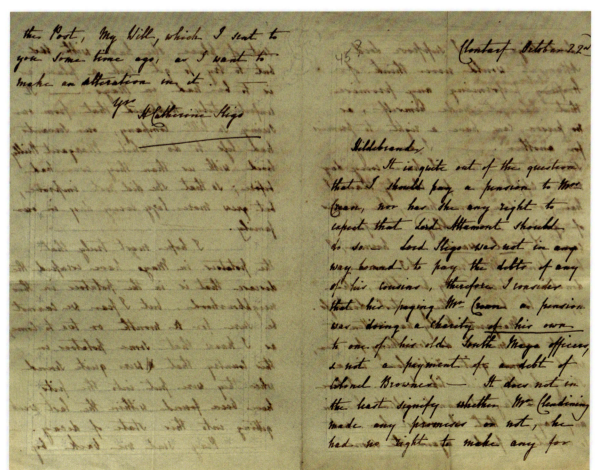

**Figure 6** | Lady Sligo Letter

EJECTMENT OF IRISH TENANTRY.

THE EJECTMENT.

**Figure 7** | "Ejectment of Irish Tenantry" (*ILN*, December 16, 1848)

The change to Poor Law relief placed a heavy burden on people whose resources were much diminished. In recognition of this difficulty, the 22 poorest unions were officially designated "distressed" and were to be offered minimal support from the Treasury. A controversial aspect of the new legislation was the "Quarter-Acre Clause," which deemed that anybody who occupied more than this amount of land was not eligible to receive government relief. Smallholders who had held onto their land during the previous two years of shortages were now forced to vacate it if they wanted Poor Law relief. In a letter to Prime Minister Russell, dated May 20, 1848, Lord Palmerston, an Irish landowner and a member of the government, explained the motivation for such harsh requirements thus: "It is useless to describe the truth that any great improvement in the social system in Ireland must be founded on an extensive change in the present state of agrarian occupation, and that this change implies a long, continued and systematic ejectment of small holders and squatting cottiers" (qtd. in Gooch 225). This harsh new relief requirement was an indication that rather than simply save lives, a secondary purpose of the government was to bring about social change in Ireland. This measure contributed to the large-scale abandonment of small properties after 1847, which added greatly to the existing dislocation and despair of the poorer classes.

Other changes were taking place in land occupancy as a result of the relief policies introduced by the British government. After August 1847, much of the financial burden for financing the amended Poor Law fell on landowners. While a number used the nonpayment of rent as an excuse to implement large-scale evictions and thus consolidate their estates, others struggled to meet the heavy financial burdens placed on them. For some policymakers in London, Irish landowners were just as much a barrier to economic progress as the potato growers at the other end of the social scale (*Times,* October 10, 1847). To clear Ireland of these indebted proprietors, in 1848 and 1849, the Encumbered Estates Acts were passed, which forced landowners who were in debt and unable to meet their financial obligations to sell their properties. Overall, a social revolution was being imposed upon the Irish landscape and on Irish society.

## One outcome was large-scale evictions, which meant that homelessness, combined with hunger, became a major source of mortality after 1847.

At the end of 1847, although food supplies were more plentiful than they had been in the preceding year, the people were without the means to purchase them. Perhaps, even more worrisome, Poor Law relief—now the only relief available from the government—was inoperative in some of the poorest districts, the Quakers observing, "in many districts the provisions of the poor law, under which all destitute persons are entitled to maintenance, are very imperfectly carried out" (*Transactions*, Report of Joseph Bewley and Jonathan Pim, December 1, 1847: 146). Asenath Nicholson noted the changes in Irish workhouses since the commencement of the food shortages.

*Before the famine they were many of them quite interesting objects for a stranger to visit, generally kept clean, not crowded and the food sufficient. But when the famine advanced, when funds decreased, when the doors were besieged by imploring applicants, who wanted a place to die so that they might be buried in a coffin, they were little else than charnel houses, while the living, shivering skeletons that squatted upon the floors, or stood with arms folded against the wall, half-clad, with hair uncombed, hands and face unwashed, added a horror if not a terror to the sight* (166).

The funds of the Quakers, however, like other private charities were almost exhausted by the end of 1847.

The beginning of 1848 brought little respite from suffering for the poor, with a higher number of applications for Poor Law relief occurring in February than in January. The distress was exacerbated by the spread of disease, especially typhus fever, and by the inclement weather. In 1848, Count Strzelecki of the British Relief Association reported that the condition of the poor in parts of Connacht and Munster was worse than in the previous two years. He estimated that 99,000 holders of land had been evicted and were homeless. Many of them did not want to

Encumbered Estates Acts were passed, which forced landowners who were in debt and unable to meet their financial obligations to sell their properties

take shelter in the workhouse due to the policy of "domestic separation," that is, the forcible separation of family members within these institutions. Instead, they applied for outdoor relief, even though they had no homes (*The Nation*, October 26, 1849). Strzelecki had been in Ireland since January 1847 and had witnessed much suffering. Yet, on 12 March 1848, the usually moderate Strzelecki reported: "The Inspectors of Ballina and Belmullet write to me that, notwithstanding all their efforts, this district is a disgrace to any civilized country" (*Report of the British Relief Association* 135). Clearly, in 1848, the Famine was far from over.

## BLACK '49

Blight reappeared on the potato crop of 1848, although other food produced was healthy. Nonetheless, a fourth year of shortages, combined with widespread disease and extensive homelessness, kept pressure on the strained resources of the Poor Law. Unlike two years earlier, however, there was little charitable money to prop up the government's relief measures.

a fourth year of shortages, combined with widespread disease and extensive homelessness, kept pressure on the strained resources of the Poor Law

Reluctantly, in February 1849, the government made a small grant of £50,000 to assist the poorest districts in Ireland. At the same time, they made it clear that no further public money would be given to Ireland. In the succeeding months, however, the distress in parts of unions in Connacht and Munster proved to be even more severe than in 1847. The suffering was exacerbated by homelessness. The government in London could have been in no doubt about the situation, with even the unsympathetic *Times* reporting on the continuing misery:

*While hundreds of thousands were deprived of food and health by the failure of the potato crop, about 90,000 holders of land had lost their hearths by evictions and voluntary surrender and become houseless, some taking refuge in the workhouses—others took outdoor relief— in a state of emaciation, sickness and nudity hardly credible* (October 19, 1849).

Clearly, the poorest districts in Ireland required external assistance, but just as clearly, the government was not willing to provide any more financial support. The solution was the introduction of the Rate in Aid tax, which levied an additional rate on all Poor Law Unions, for redistribution to the poorest ones. It was an unpopular measure in Ireland. It also showed that, despite the existence of the Act of Union, at the time of unquestionable need, the Irish people were to be left to their own resources. The despair that followed this measure was not confined to Irish people. On April 28, 1849, the Lord Lieutenant of Ireland, Lord Clarendon, privately confided to the Prime Minister, "I do not think there is another legislature in Europe that would disregard such suffering as now exists in the west of Ireland, or coldly persist in a policy of extermination."[18] The emotional appeal of the government's representative in Ireland made no difference, as no more money was to be forthcoming from the British Treasury.

In June 1849, as distress showed no signs of abating, a number of British politicians, together with the Queen, raised a private subscription for the Irish poor, which was entrusted to Count Strzelecki. In that month alone, there were 200,000 inmates in the workhouses, 770,000 people were receiving outdoor relief and 25,000 were in workhouse infirmaries. The reports from the western districts made harrowing reading, with even people in receipt of outdoor relief being described as: 'crowding together and crouching under heaps of rotten straw of their unroofed cabins, under bridges, burrowing on the roadside, or in the ditches of the cold and wet bogs" (*The Nation*, October 27, 1849).

Figure 8  |  Charlotte Kelly, *A Quiet Place Now*

# THE FAMINE KILLED EVERYTHING

Although there was some appearance of blight on the potato crops of 1850 and 1851, it was increasingly becoming limited to districts in the west of the country. It was not until 1852 that the blight fully disappeared from Ireland. By this time, the population had fallen by over 25 percent. What made the tragedy more lamentable was the fact that, since 1800, Ireland had been part of the United Kingdom, which was at the center of the vast, powerful and resource-rich British Empire. Unfortunately, the resources of that Empire had not been deployed to mitigate the sufferings of the poor in Ireland. While thousands of people, many of whom with no direct connection with Ireland, had come to the rescue of the starving poor by providing private charity, most of these donations had been concentrated in 1847.

The impact of seven years of food shortages continued to resonate well beyond 1852. Even after good harvests had returned to the country, the Irish population continued to fall. In 1841, the population of Ireland had been in excess of 8 million; by 1901, it had fallen to a little more than 4 million. At the beginning of the 21st century, it still remained smaller than it had been in 1845. Using this simple demographic measure, it is possible to see that Ireland never recovered from the tragedy of the Great Hunger. However, beyond the loss of population, much more was lost in those dark years, losses that are more difficult to quantify or to describe. In the words of Máire Ní Grianna, descended from a Famine survivor from County Donegal: "Poetry, music and dancing died ... The Famine killed everything" (Deane 204) **[Figure 8]**.

# CHRONOLOGY OF THE GREAT HUNGER

## 1845

| | |
|---|---|
| August | A new disease, increasingly referred to as blight, was damaging potato crops in parts of mainland Europe and appeared to be spreading westwards. It was first recorded in Ireland at the Botanic Gardens in Dublin on August 20th. |
| September | The blight was sighted in many parts of Ireland, although its appearance was patchy. The affected potatoes were inedible. |
| October | The British Prime Minister, Sir Robert Peel, appointed a Scientific Commission to inquire into the cause of the disease and find a remedy. It was unsuccessful. |
| November | Potato shortages were causing food prices to rise. Workhouses were allowed to provide alternatives to potatoes to the inmates. |
| | Indian corn was imported from the U.S. for sale and free distribution to the poor. |
| | A temporary Relief Commission was appointed in Dublin to oversee local relief efforts. |
| December | The Irish Board of Works was asked to assist in providing relief by organizing employment for the destitute on public works schemes. |

## 1846

| | |
|---|---|
| January | Disease was spreading in Ireland, especially dysentery, fever and diarrhea, caused by eating rotten potatoes or uncooked grain. |
| March | A Fever Act established a temporary Board of Health in Dublin. |
| June | Sir Robert Peel resigned as Prime Minister, having lost the support of his party over the repeal of the Corn Laws. |
| July | Lord John Russell and his Whig Party formed a new government. |
| | Reports of the re-appearance of the potato blight were increasing. |
| August | A new, harsher system of public works was introduced, with wages more tightly regulated. |
| September | The potato disease returned and spread rapidly, destroying more of the crop than in the previous year. |
| November | Deaths from famine were being recorded, although no official list of mortality was ever kept. |
| December | The small town of Skibbereen in County Cork achieved international notoriety for the scale of disease and death occurring there daily. |
| | By the end of the year, over half of the workhouses in Ireland were full. |

# 1847

| | |
|---|---|
| January | Despite delays and problems in opening the public works schemes, over 600,000 people were employed on them for a minimal wage. |
| | A number of private individuals formed committees to help the Irish poor. The largest charitable organization was the British Relief Association, which had its headquarters in London. |
| | Changes in government relief were announced: the public works were to be phased out and government soup kitchens were to be opened. |
| March | The public works started to close down with workers being discharged. |
| May | Government soup kitchens opened throughout the country, but with some delays and reports of poor quality soup. |
| July | Over three million people were being fed daily in the government soup kitchens. |
| | Although the new potato harvest was relatively blight-free, the crop was small. |
| August | Soup kitchens are closed down. The Poor Law Amendment Act is passed, which transferred the responsibility for all relief to the workhouse system. It also provided for more workhouses to be built. |
| November | Denis Mahon, a landowner in Strokestown, County Roscommon, was shot dead. He had evicted large numbers of his tenants. |
| December | The change to Poor Law relief not only had failed to save lives, but also had contributed to an increase in evictions and emigration. An estimated 220,000 left Ireland in 1847. |

# 1848

| | |
|---|---|
| February | Almost 200,000 people were receiving relief in the workhouses; almost 500,000 were receiving outdoor relief. |
| April | Over 600,000 people were receiving outdoor relief. Evictions and emigration were also increasing, but no central records were kept. |
| June | Over 200 female orphans, who had been inmates of the workhouses, sailed for Australia. Hundreds more were to follow them. |
| July | Potato blight spotted in parts of the west; parts of the north east were reporting healthy crops. |
| | At the end of the month, a nationalist group known as Young Ireland led a small, unsuccessful rebellion against British rule. |
| August | The first Encumbered Estates Act was passed to facilitate the sale of land that was heavily mortgaged. |
| November | Many of the poorest Poor Law workhouses were in debt, but as many as 3,000 people were applying for relief daily. |
| December | Cholera appeared in some parts of Ireland, adding to the already high death toll from disease. An estimated 180,000 emigrated in 1848. |

## 1849

| | |
|---|---|
| February | To assist the struggling Poor Law, the British government made a grant of £50,000 available. |
| April | The recent government grant was already exhausted and the Poor Law Commissioners were without funds. |
| May | A new Irish tax was introduced, the Rate-in-Aid, which was intended to support the poorest workhouses. |
| July | Almost 800,000 people were in receipt of outdoor relief. |
| | A second Encumbered Estates Act was passed. |
| August | Queen Victoria and her family visited Ireland. Overall, they were warmly received. |
| | Some blight was evident, but mostly in the west. |
| December | During this year, the number of evicted families totaled almost 17,000, while an estimated 220,000 emigrated. |

## 1850

| | |
|---|---|
| February | Following complaints about the orphan girls being sent to Australia, an inquiry was held. |
| May | Over one million people were receiving both workhouse and outdoor relief. |
| August | There were only limited instances of blight on the potato crop, mostly in the southwest of the country. |
| | Approximately 210,000 people emigrated in 1850. |

## 1851

| | |
|---|---|
| March | The census was taken. It recorded that the Irish population had fallen from 8,175,124 people in 1841, to 6,552,385. |
| August | The potato crop was largely blight-free. |
| | An estimated 250,000 had emigrated during the year. |

## 1852

Although the Great Hunger was widely considered to be "over," levels of eviction and emigration remained high.

## 1901

The population was 4,458,775.

# ENDNOTES

[1] See David Valone and Christine Kinealy (2002) for a discussion of the renewed academic engagement with the Great Hunger.

[2] For further details of charitable response to subsistence crises in Ireland see Kinealy (2013).

[3] The most comprehensive overview of this earlier famine is provided in David Dickson, Arctic Ireland: The Extraordinary Story of the Great Frost and Forgotten Famine of 1740–41.

[4] Terrence McDonough, *Was Ireland a Colony? Economics, Politics and Culture in Nineteenth-Century Ireland* (2005).

[5] *Eighth Annual Report of Poor Law Commissioners for England and Ireland* (1846).

[6] Geraint Parry, Hillel Steiner and Andrew Marrison (eds), *Freedom and Trade: Free Trade and its Reception, 1815–1960*: 50.

[7] This point is made in Peter Gray, *Famine, Land and Politics: British Government and Irish Society, 1843–1850*.

[8] Christine Kinealy, A Death-Dealing Famine. The Great Hunger in Ireland: 138.

[9] Christine Kinealy, *Charity and the Great Hunger in Ireland. The Kindness of Strangers* (2013): ch. 9.

[10] Ibid. For the role of the Society of Friends during the Great Hunger see ch. 3.

[11] Asenath Nicholson, *Annals of the Famine in Ireland, in 1847, 1848, and 1849:* 143.

[12] Kinealy (2013): 172.

[13] Ibid., chap.7.

[14] For more on this debate see, Gerard Moran, *Sending Out Ireland's Poor: Assisted Emigration to North America in the Nineteenth Century*.

[15] Lord Sligo to Lord Monteagle, 8 October 1848, Monteagle Papers.

[16] *Papers Relating to Proceedings for Relief of Distress, and State of Unions and Workhouses in Ireland*, 1848, fifth series, January 4, 1848: 368.

[17] *Papers Relating to Proceedings for Relief of Distress, and State of Unions and Workhouses in Ireland*, 1848, sixth series, 25 March 1848: 63.

[18] Lord Clarendon to Lord John Russell, 28 April 1849, Clarendon Papers.

# WORKS CITED

## GOVERNMENT PUBLICATIONS

*Eighth Annual Report of Poor Law Commissioners for England and Ireland.* London: Poor Law Commission Office. 1846. Print.

*Hansard.* House of Commons Debate. August 17, 1846. Lord John Russell. 772–78. Print.

Monteagle Papers, Ms.13,398, National Library of Ireland.

*Papers Relating to Proceedings for Relief of Distress, and State of Unions and Workhouses in Ireland.* British Parliamentary Papers. 1848 fifth series (919) iv. Print.

*Papers Relating to Proceedings for Relief of Distress, and State of Unions and Workhouses in Ireland.* British Parliamentary Papers. 1848 sixth series (955) lvi. Print.

*Report of the British Relief Association for the Relief of Extreme Distress in Ireland and Scotland.* London: Richard Clay, 1849. Print.

*Report of the Select Committee Appointed to Consider Emigration from the UK.* British Parliamentary Papers. 1826/27 (550) v. Print.

*Russell Papers* (Papers of Lord John Russell). National Archives, London. PRO 30/22. Print.


## PRIMARY AND SECONDARY SOURCES

Bennett, William. *Narrative of a Recent Journey of Six Weeks in Ireland, in Connexion with the Subject of Supplying Small Seed to Some of the Remoter Districts.* London: Charles Gilpin, 1847. Print.

Clarendon Papers. Irish Letter-Books. Bodleian Library. Oxford. Print.

*Connaught Telegraph.* Mayo. "The Marquis of Sligo." July 22, 1846. Print.

---."Sir Roger Palmer". July 5, 1848. Print.

Crowley, John, William J. Smyth, Mike Murphy, eds. *Atlas of the Great Irish Famine.* Cork: Cork University Press, 2012. Print.

Deane, Emer, trans. "Memories of the Famine." *The Field Day Anthology of Irish Writing*, 3 vols. Ed. Seamus Deane, Derry: Field Day Publications, 1991. Vol. 2. 203–04. Print.

Dickson, David. *Arctic Ireland: The Extraordinary Story of the Great Frost and Forgotten Famine of 1740–41.* Belfast: White Row Press, 1997. Print.

*Dublin Evening Mail.* Dublin. "State of the Country." April 7, 1847. Print.

Feehan, John. "The Potato: Root of the Famine." *Atlas of the Great Irish Famine.* Eds. John Crowley, William J. Smyth, Mike Murphy. Cork: Cork University Press, 2012. 28–37. Print.

*Gardeners' Chronicle and Gazette.* London. "We Stop the Press ..." September 13, 1845. Print.

Gray, Peter. *Famine, Land and Politics: British Government and Irish Society, 1843–1850.* Dublin and Portland, OR: Irish Academic Press, 1999. Print.

Gooch, George Peabody. *The Later Correspondence of Lord John Russell.* London: Longmans and Green, 1925. Print.

*The Illustrated London News.* London. "Sketches in the West of Ireland." February 13, 1847. Print.

*The Independent.* London. "Blair Issues Apology for Irish Potato Famine." June 2, 1997. Print.

Kennedy, Liam and Leslie A. Clarkson. "Birth, Death and Exile: Irish Population History, 1700–1921." B. J. Graham and L. J. Proudfoot, eds. *An Historical Geography of Ireland.* London: Academic Press, 1993. Print.

Kinealy, Christine. *A Death-Dealing Famine. The Great Hunger in Ireland.* London: Pluto Press, 1997. Print.

---. *Charity and the Great Hunger in Ireland: The Kindness of Strangers.* London: Bloomsbury Press, 2013. Print.

McDonough, Terrence. *Was Ireland a Colony? Economics, Politics and Culture in Nineteenth-Century Ireland.* Dublin: Irish Academic Press, 2005. Print.

Malthus, Thomas. *An Essay on The Principle of Population, as It Affects the Future Improvement of Society.* London: J. Johnson, 1798. Print.

Moran, Gerard. *Sending Out Ireland's Poor: Assisted Emigration to North America in the Nineteenth Century.* Dublin: Four Courts Press, 2004. Print.

*The Nation.* Dublin. "Domestic News." November 27, 1846. Print.

---. "Meeting of Irish Peers and MPs." January 15, 1847. Print.

---. "The Provinces – The Harvest." July 21, 1847. Print.

---. "Expenditure in the Relief of Irish Distress." October 26, 1849. Print.

*New York Christian Advocate.* New York. "News from Europe." July 21, 1847. Print.

Nicholls, George. *A History of the Irish Poor Law: in Connexion with the Condition of the People.* London: J. Murray, 1856. Print.

Nicholson, Asenath. *Annals of the Famine in Ireland, in 1847, 1848, and 1849.* New York: E. French, 1851. Print.

Ó Gráda, Cormac. *Ireland's Great Famine: An Overview.* Dublin: Centre for Economic Research, working paper series, 2004. Print.

*The Observer Magazine.* London. "Feeding off History." February 20, 1994. Print.

Parry, Geraint, Hillel Steiner and Andrew Marrison, eds. *Freedom and Trade: Free Trade and its Reception, 1815–1960.* London: Routledge, 1998. Print.

The *Times.* London. "Ireland." Decemeber 24, 1846. Print.

---. "State of Ireland." March 24, 1847. Print.

---. "Ireland." October 10, 1847. Print.

---. "State of Ireland." October 19, 1849. Print.

*Transactions of the Central Relief Committee of the Society of Friends During the Famine in Ireland, in 1846 and 1847.* Dublin: Hodges and Smith, 1852. Print.

Valone, David and Christine Kinealy, eds. *Ireland's Great Hunger: Silence, Memory, and Commemoration.* Lanham, MD: University Press of America, 2002. Print.

# IMAGES

**Cover**

Kieran Tuohy
b. 1953

*Lonely Widow*
2005
Bog oak
62 x 15 x 14 in
© 2005 Kieran Tuohy

**Figure 1**

John Behan
b. 1938

*The Arrival—The New Dawn*
2000
Cast Bronze
21.5 x 22 x 15.5 in
© 2000 John Behan

**Figure 2**

John Behan
b. 1938

*Potatoes: Famine*
2000
Cast Bronze
21.5 x 22 x 15.5 in
© 2000 John Behan

**Figure 3**

"Map of Poor Law Unions"
page 123

*Atlas of the Great Irish Famine*
1845–52
Edited by
John Crowley,
William J. Smyth
Mike Murphy
UCC

**Figure 4**

James Mahony

"The Central Soup Depot,
Barrack-Street, Cork"
*The Illustrated London News*
March 13, 1847

**Figure 5**

Margaret Lyster Chamberlain
b. 1954

*The Leave-Taking*
2000
Cast bronze
25 x 36 x 12 in
© 2000 Margaret Lyster Chamberlain

**Figure 6**

Lady Sligo Letter

**Figure 7**

Fitzpatrick

"Ejectment of Irish Tenantry"
*The Illustrated London News*
December 16, 1848

**Figure 8**

Charlotte Kelly
b. 1960

*A Quiet Place Now*
2009
Oil on canvas
24 x 36 in
© 2009 Charlotte Kelly

Images provided by
Ireland's Great Hunger Museum,
Quinnipiac University unless
noted otherwise.

## ABOUT THE AUTHOR

Christine Kinealy writes on modern Ireland, with a focus on the Great Hunger. Publications include *This Great Calamity; The Irish Famine 1845-52* (1994); *Repeal and Revolution. 1848 in Ireland* (2009); *Daniel O'Connell and Abolition. The Saddest People the Sun Sees* (2011); *Charity and the Great Hunger in Ireland: The Kindness of Strangers* (2013). She is the founding Director of Ireland's Great Hunger Institute at Quinnipiac University in Connecticut.

**IRELAND'S GREAT HUNGER** MUSEUM | QUINNIPIAC UNIVERSITY PRESS ©2014

**SERIES EDITORS**

Niamh O'Sullivan
Grace Brady

**IMAGE RESEARCH**

Claire Tynan

**DESIGN / PRODUCTION MANAGEMENT**

Group C Inc, New Haven
Jessica Cassettari
Brad Collins

**ACKNOWLEDGMENT**

Office of Public Affairs, Quinnipiac University

**PUBLISHER**

Quinnipiac University Press

**PRINTING**

GHP Media

ISBN 978-0-9904686-1-5

**Ireland's Great Hunger** Museum
Quinnipiac University

3011 Whitney Avenue
Hamden, CT 06518-1908
203-582-6500

**www.ighm.org**